NAKED MOLE RATS

Emma Bassier

DiscoverRoo
An Imprint of Pop!
popbooksonline.com

abdobooks.com

Published by Pop!, a division of ABDO, PO Box 398166, Minneapolis, Minnesota 55439. Copyright © 2020 by POP, LLC. International copyrights reserved in all countries. No part of this book may be reproduced in any form without written permission from the publisher. Pop!™ is a trademark and logo of POP, LLC.

Printed in the United States of America, North Mankato, Minnesota.

102019
012020

THIS BOOK CONTAINS RECYCLED MATERIALS

Cover Photo: Joel Sartore/National Geographic Image Collection/Getty Images

Interior Photos: Joel Sartore/National Geographic Image Collection/Getty Images, 1; Frans Lanting/MINT Images/ Science Source, 5; Gregory G. Dimijian/Science Source, 6, 18; Red Line Editorial, 7; H. Schmidbauer/picture alliance/ blickwinkel/H/Newscom, 8–9; Joerg Sarbach/AP Images, 11, 30; Shutterstock Images, 12, 13, 14–15, 17, 21, 25, 26–27, 28, 29 (bottom), 31; Steve Gorton/DK Images, 19; iStockphoto, 20; CB2/ZOB/WENN.com/Newscom, 23; Mark Bowler/ NHPA/Photoshot/Newscom, 24; K. Wothe/picture alliance/ blickwinkel/K/Newscom, 29 (top); Wade Payne/AP Images, 29 (middle)

Editor: Nick Rebman
Series Designer: Jake Slavik

Library of Congress Control Number: 2019942420

Publisher's Cataloging-in-Publication Data

Names: Bassier, Emma, author.

Title: Naked mole rats / by Emma Bassier

Description: Minneapolis, Minnesota : Pop!, 2020 | Series: Weird and wonderful animals | Includes online resources and index.

Identifiers: ISBN 9781532166075 (lib. bdg.) | ISBN 9781644943373 (pbk.) | ISBN 9781532167393 (ebook)

Subjects: LCSH: Naked mole rat--Juvenile literature. | Rodents--Behavior--Juvenile literature. | Oddities-- Juvenile literature. | Burrowing animals --Juvenile literature. | Mammals --Juvenile literature.

Classification: DDC 599.359--dc23

Pop open this book and you'll find QR codes loaded with information, so you can learn even more!

Scan this code* and others like it while you read, or visit the website below to make this book pop!

popbooksonline.com/naked-mole-rats

*Scanning QR codes requires a web-enabled smart device with a QR code reader app and a camera.

TABLE OF CONTENTS

WRINKLY DIGGERS

A pinkish-gray body wiggles down a dark hole. A naked mole rat is digging a tunnel in the ground. It shares the tunnel with other naked mole rats. Most naked mole rats spend lots of time digging.

Naked mole rats look for food
while they dig.

Naked mole rats are rodents.

Rodents are a type of **mammal** with sharp front teeth that never stop growing. Naked mole rats live in dry grasslands in East Africa.

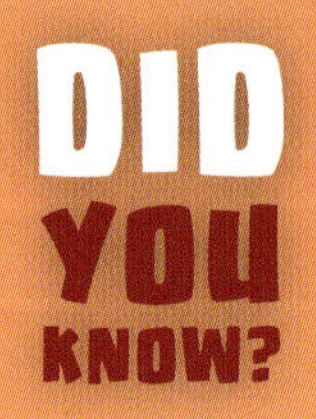

Naked mole rats are more closely related to porcupines than they are to moles or rats.

RANGE MAP

SOMALIA
ETHIOPIA
KENYA
INDIAN
OCEAN
Naked mole rat range
N
W E
S

During the daytime, the temperature above ground can be very hot. The temperature is more comfortable underground where naked mole rats live. Naked mole rats live in burrows. A burrow is a hole in the ground.

Naked mole rats' burrows are made up of several rooms connected by tunnels. This underground **habitat** keeps naked mole rats safe from **predators**. It also saves them from getting sunburned.

STRONG JAWS

A naked mole rat weighs up to 2 ounces (57 g). The animal's jaws are very strong. Its body is 3 to 4 inches (8–10 cm) long. However, the tail adds up to 3 inches (8 cm) to a naked mole rat's length.

A naked mole rat uses many muscles when it closes its jaws.

A naked mole rat emerges from its burrow.

A naked mole rat has a short, wide

head. Large front teeth stick out of

its mouth. The animal chews on hard

objects every day. Constant chewing keeps the teeth from getting too long.

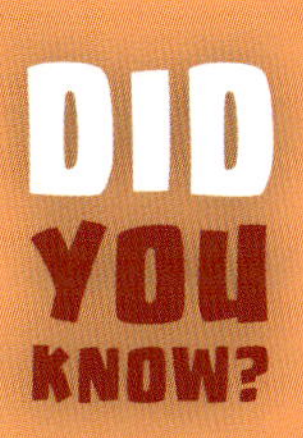

Naked mole rats can move their front teeth independently. They can spread them apart and bring them back together.

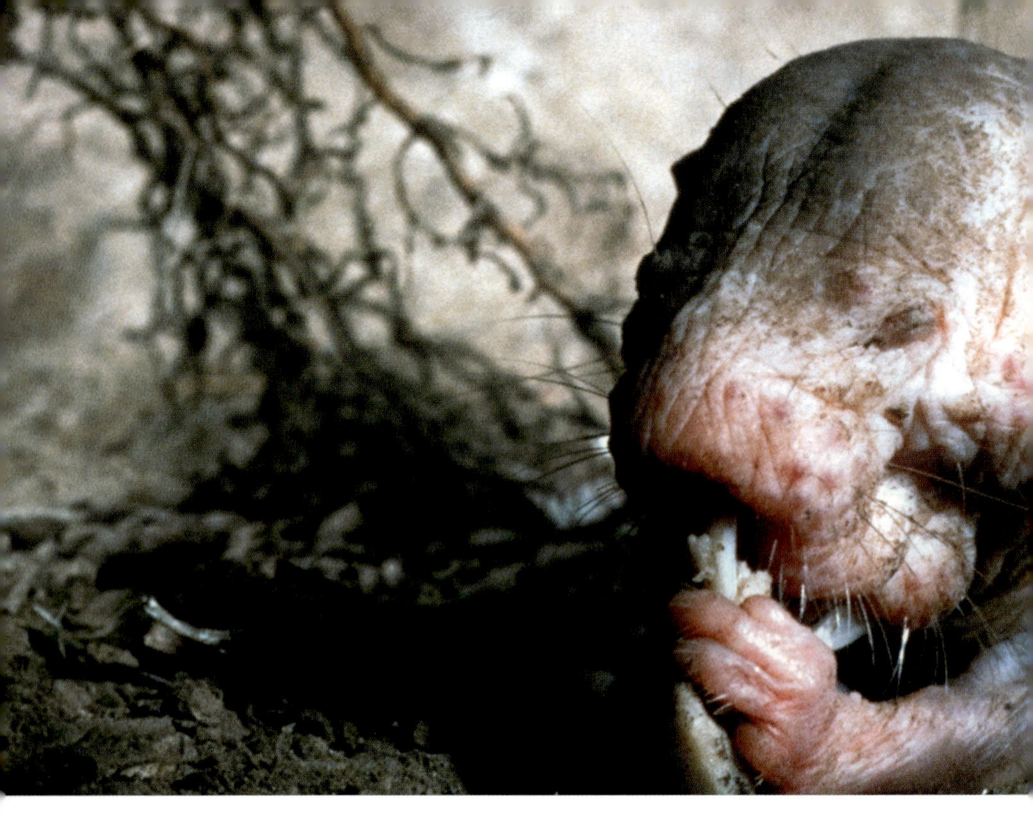

A naked mole rat is nearly hairless.

However, the animal has approximately

100 fine hairs on its body. Naked mole

rats have tiny eyes. They do not see well.

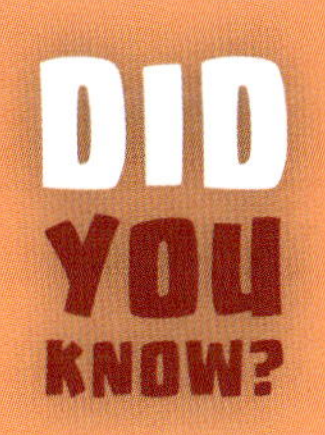

A naked mole rat gnaws on a piece of food.

Instead, naked mole rats rely on their senses of smell and touch.

DID YOU KNOW? Naked mole rats can make 18 different sounds to communicate.

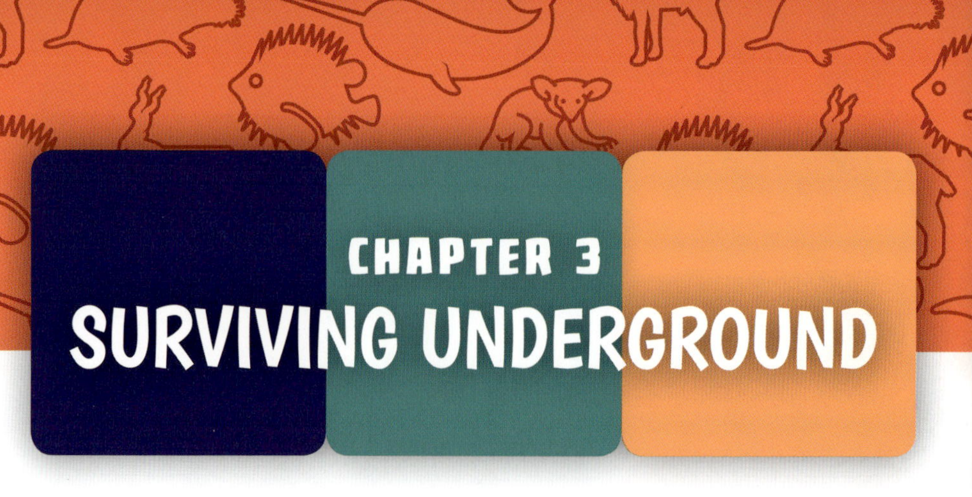

Underground **habitats** are dark. Naked mole rats use the fine hairs on their bodies to feel what is around them. These hairs help them notice airflow and ground movements. Naked mole rats

also have stretchy skin. It helps them

turn around in tight spaces.

Naked mole rats dig with strong jaws and teeth. Their lips close behind their teeth. This stops dirt from getting into their mouths.

Naked mole rats eat mostly roots.

But they also eat their own poop. The

poop may still have nutrients in it.

A naked mole rat's jaws are strong enough to chew through concrete.

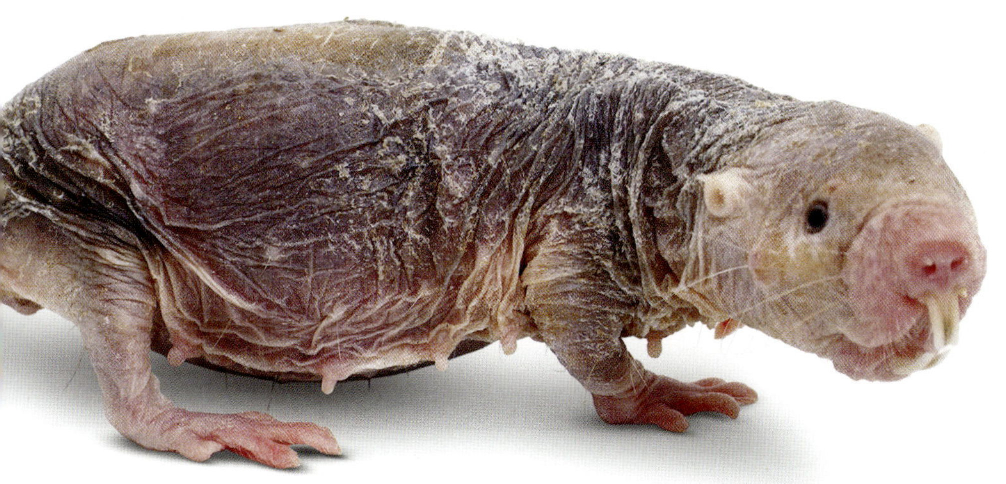

Naked mole rats have few **predators** underground. From time to time, snakes may try to eat them. Also,

naked mole rats from other **colonies** may compete with them for space and food.

Naked mole rats roll around in their poop. As a result, every animal in the colony smells the same. They know not to attack one another. If other naked mole rats enter the burrow, they will smell different. The members of the colony will know they are **intruders**.

A naked mole rat guards the entrance to its burrow.

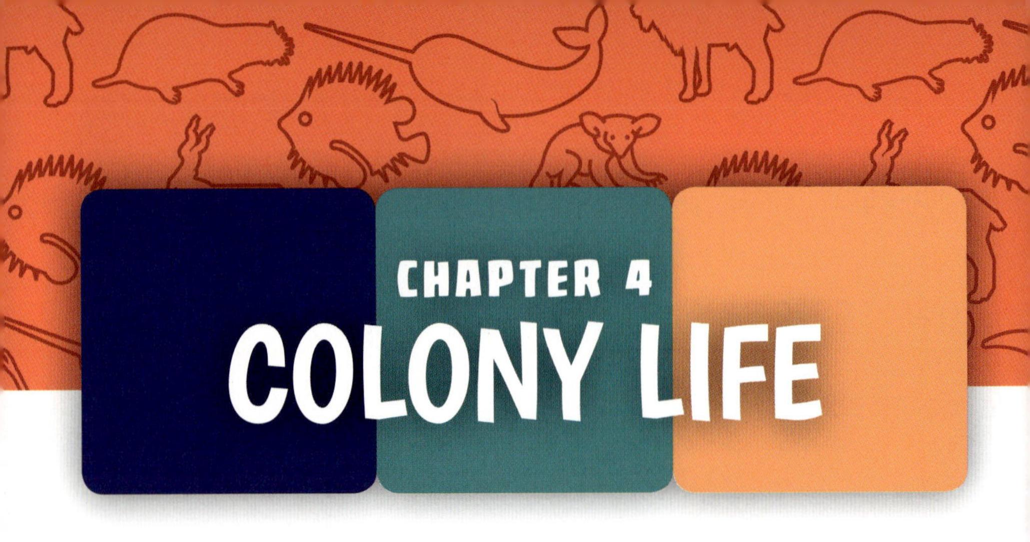

A burrow can have 2.5 miles (4.0 km) of tunnels. The tunnels are 1.5 inches (3.8 cm) wide. Each room in the burrow has a purpose. The burrow has rooms

for eating, storing food, and pooping.

One room is a nursery for the **pups**.

Each member of the **colony** has a

specific job. One female is in charge. She

is the queen. She is larger than the other

naked mole rats. She is the only female

who mates.

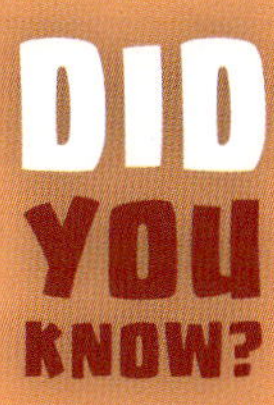

Insects such as ants and bees live in colonies. But colony behavior is unusual for **mammals.**

A naked mole rat walks through its burrow.

Most members of the colony are
workers. They look for food and dig
tunnels. Some members are soldiers.
They protect the colony from attacks.

To do so, they pile up their bodies and block **predators** from entering the burrow. They also fight with their sharp teeth.

LIFE CYCLE OF A NAKED MOLE RAT

A worker cleans each pup and takes it to the nursery. The queen nurses the pups there for a few weeks.

The queen gives birth to pups. She can have more than 25 at one time.

After a few months, the pups become workers or soldiers.

After one year, pups are fully grown.

Scientists don't know how long naked mole rats live in the wild. But the animals can live up to 30 years in zoos.

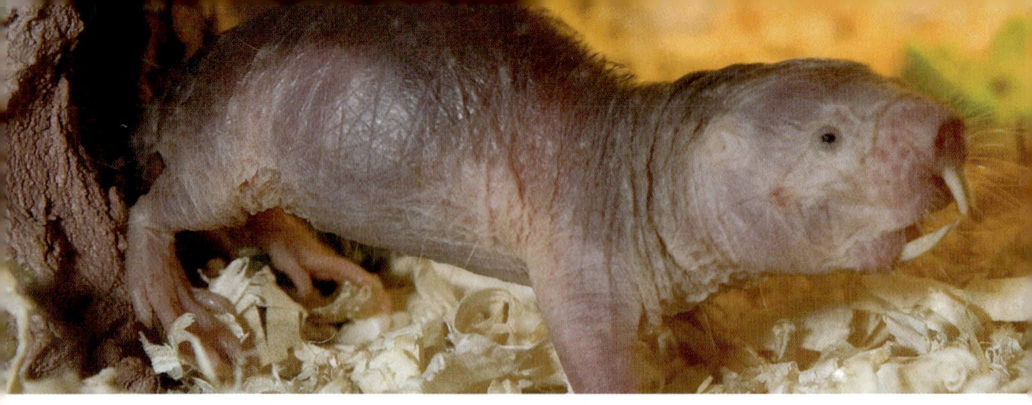

MAKING CONNECTIONS

TEXT-TO-SELF

Would you want to hold a naked mole rat? Why or why not?

TEXT-TO-TEXT

Have you read other books about animals that live underground? How are those animals similar to and different from naked mole rats?

TEXT-TO-WORLD

Naked mole rats have certain body parts that help them live underground. What are some human body parts that help people live above ground?

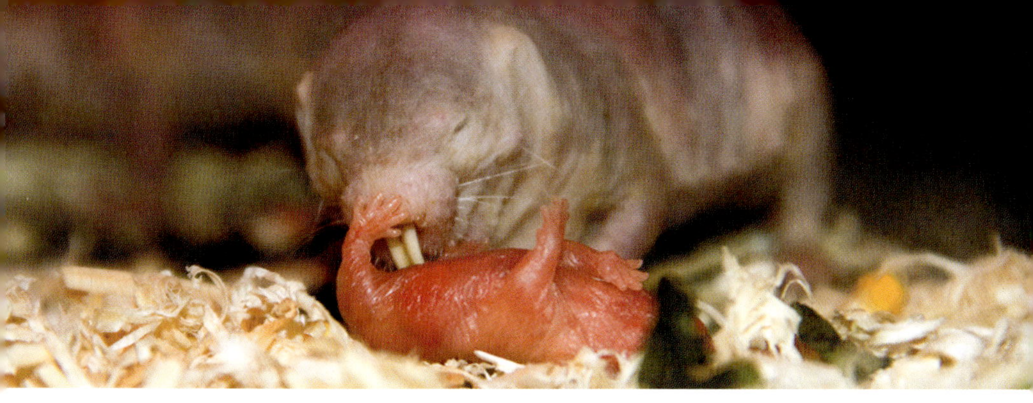

GLOSSARY

colony – a group of animals that live together.

habitat – the area where an animal normally lives.

intruder – an animal that enters another animal's living space by force.

mammal – a type of animal that has hair or fur and feeds milk to its young.

predator – an animal that hunts other animals for food.

pup – a baby naked mole rat.

INDEX

ONLINE RESOURCES
popbooksonline.com

Scan this code* and others like it while you read, or visit the website below to make this book pop!

popbooksonline.com/naked-mole-rats

*Scanning QR codes requires a web-enabled smart device with a QR code reader app and a camera.